POCKET BOOK OF
ONE-LINERS

EXEMPLARY EXCUSES

ALLSORTED.

An exclusive edition for

This edition first published in Great Britain in 2017
by Allsorted Ltd, Watford, Herts, UK WD19 4BG

Author: Roffy
Cover design: Milestone Creative
Contents layout: seagulls.net

ISBN: 978-1-910562-92-5

Printed in China

CONTENTS

INTRODUCTION

The dedicated excuse-maker starts early in life. When you were at school, did you rip up every genuine excuse note your parents ever wrote and replace it with your own forgery so the handwriting was always consistent when you needed to pen your own?

No? We didn't think so, otherwise you wouldn't need this book.

So let's get the most common excuse out of the way first. You've already heard it. You've already used it.

'It wasn't me.'

And be honest – the last time you used it, was it really an excuse or a cheeky lie? We're not here to pass judgement, though. On you or Shaggy.

What we can do is offer you over 500 premium excuses to avoid or deflect whatever life throws at you. And if they don't work? Sorry, the dog ate all our best excuses.

AT HOME

THINGS GO WRONG IN EVEN THE MOST LOVING FAMILY HOME. WHETHER IT'S WELL-INTENTIONED PLANS THAT STRAY OFF-COURSE, BAD PLANNING THAT HONESTLY HAD NO HOPE IN THE FIRST PLACE, SHEER BAD LUCK OR PLAIN OLD GETTING CAUGHT – EVERY DAY SOMETHING IS SENT TO TRY YOU.

In fact, you spend around half your life at home. Admittedly, most of that time is occupied by sleeping, but in the hours you are awake there are plenty of bullets to dodge. They may be fired from your family, your neighbours or even complete strangers that show up on your doorstep.

But the right excuse can help keep family life harmonious. If you can delay doing the washing up until after you've finished watching the box set, everybody wins. If you can get someone else to do it, well, at least *you've* won. For the moment.

EMPTY SHELVES

WHEN YOUR 'SNACK' WAS MEANT FOR TOMORROW'S DINNER.

- I didn't see your name on it.
- Wow, that was crazy. Just like in the fairy tale. What? What do you mean you didn't see the bears?
- It's not like there are none left in the shops.
- You don't like things going past the use-by date.
- I'm helping you with your diet.
- I had to eat the cheesecake because it was in the way of the juice.
- You said they were buy-one-get-one-free, so I ate the free one.
- I was making room for healthier food.
- I'm helping you support local traders.
- My body is a temple but my mouth is a committed atheist.

BOOZE LOSER

WHEN YOU'VE DRUNK THE HOUSE DRY.

- You said I should drink less lager, so I drank your vodka instead.
- Your whisky was 40 years old so it must have been going off.
- I gave in to beer pressure.
- I'm currently in the planning stages of a hangover.
- You keep telling me not to procrastinate, so I drank it all today.
- It took all your vintage wine to get rid of the taste of the ouzo.
- I'm practising for a job in quality control.
- In dog beers, I've only had one so far this evening.

RUNNING ON EMPTY

YOU BROUGHT THEIR CAR BACK IN ONE PIECE, WHAT MORE DO THEY WANT?

- There wasn't enough fuel to get to the garage.
- There was a protest against big oil companies.
- I said you should get a Tesla - then we wouldn't have this problem.
- You said you wanted the car back at 7pm - getting fuel would have made me late.
- You used more of the petrol than I did.
- I don't have enough money for clothes *and* fuel.
- I went to get petrol but I bought charcoal and foldable chairs by mistake.
- There's been a lot of car thefts recently and it would be worse if it got stolen with a full tank.

SNAP, CRUMBLE AND POP

WHY DO THINGS ONLY GET DAMAGED WHEN YOU BORROW THEM?

- The police thought it was a bomb and tried to detonate it.
- You should thank me for breaking it, it was so off-trend.
- It was like that when I borrowed it.
- I found the neighbour's kid playing with it.
- You've been looking for an excuse to buy a new one anyway.
- The parking sensor on the back of the car is broken. As is the rest of the back of the car.
- There was a terrible flood. It got everything, your underwear, everything.

SET-TOP SHOCKS

WHEN YOU'VE DELETED THEIR FAVOURITE SHOW FROM THE PLANNER.

- I'm helping you find something better to watch.
- You spend too much time on the sofa in the first place.
- If there's too much on the hard drive it will start slowing down.
- There's a rental fee if we store it on the box for too long.
- It will be on Netflix in three years.
- I thought you'd watched it.
- Surely each episode is the same anyway?
- The last episode made you cry.
- The last episode made me cry.

DODGY DIY

IF YOU ARE CONSTANTLY THINKING D-I-WHY?

- It'll have to wait, my overalls are in the wash.
- Sorry, I lent my tools to Dave. I think he moved.
- The preparation takes longer than you think.
- They sold me the wrong paint.
- I think I used a left-handed hammer by mistake.
- The bloke at the DIY store said it can't be done.
- It has to leak, otherwise the pressure builds up and it might explode.
- The colours do match, it's a trick of the light.
- I thought the tiles were meant to be temporary?
- The house is sloping, not the shelf.
- It's bad for the economy if we don't pay someone else to fix it.

KITCHEN CALAMITIES

BECAUSE TV COOKING SHOWS HAVE A LOT TO ANSWER FOR.

- The oven is broken.
- Are you sure you're hungry?
- There isn't time to tidy the kitchen first.
- It's not how it looks, it's how it tastes.
- Pinch of salt, pint of salt - who cares?
- It's your mother's recipe, perhaps she should cook it for you?
- The toaster is possessed.
- The jug is imperial but the microwave is metric.
- I thought you were allergic to vegetables?
- There's no point in cooking - the dishwasher is already full.
- I didn't go grocery shopping because I lost my loyalty card.

I COULDN'T FIND THE HIMALAYAN CHERIMOYA SEEDS THE RECIPE REQUIRED, SO I MADE TOAST INSTEAD.

THE LAST TIME I USED THE VACUUM CLEANER IT SUCKED ALL THE AIR OUT OF THE ROOM AND I PASSED OUT.

HIDING FROM HOUSEWORK

WASHING UP IS FOR LOSERS.

- I don't know how to turn the mop on.
- 90% of household dust is skin - we don't have a medical disposal licence.
- I think our neighbours steal my underwear off the washing line.
- The broom handle is too long.
- I can't find 2nd gear on the Dyson.
- If the windows are too clean they might dazzle passing motorists.
- I'm sure there's an app on my phone that can do the washing up.
- The pile of old magazines is essential for the room's feng shui.
- I can't clean that now - the mould might be a cure for something.
- I've already swept the room with a glance.

GARDENING GAFFES

GREEN FINGERS? BETTER SEE THE DOCTOR ABOUT THAT.

- Wow, it's hot out there!
- Wow, it's cold out there!
- Wow it's... OK, but it won't last.
- If I trim the hedge it will damage the ecology of the garden.
- The lawnmower is manual and I only have a licence for an automatic.
- The garden waste bin is full.
- Some of the weeds are prettier than the flowers.
- The grass is too long for the mower but too short for the strimmer.
- It's not the right time of year to plant/tend/harvest.
- There are baby birds in the tree. You don't want me to scare the mummy away, do you?
- If we grow our own vegetables, we'll be banned from the supermarket.

ANNIVER-SORRY

CAREFUL - EVEN YOU KNOW MAKING EXCUSES HERE WILL MOST LIKELY MAKE IT WORSE.

- I was making sure you remembered first - I didn't want you to be embarrassed.
- The more important anniversary is the day we met.
- But every day is special with you.
- I recently suffered a significant head injury.
- It's also the day my first dog died. Painful memories. Painful.
- I didn't want to remind you how old we really are.
- How am I to remember time passes when, with you, it stands still?
- It's our copper anniversary - you know how it turns your skin green.
- I just haven't been able to think of a gift worthy of you.

DIRTY CACHE

WHEN YOU FORGOT TO CLEAR YOUR INTERNET HISTORY.

- There was a power surge and it just appeared.
- I was searching for pictures of a wet cat.
- Big Richard is my friend's nickname.
- Nothing to do with me - this laptop is second hand.
- It's research for a documentary I'm making.
- The charity website I was donating to must have been hacked.
- Don't look at me, this is your laptop.

PLAYING AWAY

IF YOU NEED ANY OF THESE EXCUSES, YOU'LL GET WHAT YOU DESERVE.

- She's my massage therapist.
- The mattress company sent them to check the bedsprings.
- Those aren't text messages from your sister. It's the latest instalment of my Kindle romance novel.
- It's not a love bite. I was vacuuming and the hose got stuck to my neck.
- Those aren't long blonde hairs on my coat. A sheep dog jumped up on me.
- That's not lipstick on the glass. I bit my lip and it was bleeding.
- I wasn't staring at her bottom. I was trying to see what jeans those are because you would look great in them.
- Yes, it was a woman's voice on the phone. She wanted to know if I had suffered a workplace injury in the last year.

CIRCUMVENTING SHOPPING

BECAUSE IT DOESN'T TAKE TWO PEOPLE TO SHOP.

- Surely it's cheaper online?
- Your coupons have all expired.
- You know I get trolley rage.
- I do not subscribe to the consumerist society.
- It's always busy at this time of day.
- I thought we were adopting a minimalist lifestyle?
- The frozen food department gives me Seasonal Affective Disorder.
- The supermarket told me to BOGOF last time.

BUYER'S REMORSE

WHAT HAVE YOU JUST BOUGHT? A MOTORBIKE? AN X-BOX? A 200-INCH TV WITH INTEGRATED SANDWICH MAKER?

- It was 50% off!
- But I neeeeeeed it.
- We discussed it last week.
- It's still cheaper than your shoe collection.
- The last 50 things I bought were for you.
- Surely you can see the benefits?
- I'm happy to buy you one as well.
- The salesperson looked unhappy - I just bought it to make their day.
- We can start saving now for a better holiday next year.

LONGING FOR LIE-INS

GETTING OUT OF BED MEANS STARTING THE DAY. AND WE DON'T WANT THAT, DO WE?

- You said I'd regret it in the morning, so I slept until noon.
- It would look weird if I wore my pyjamas all day anywhere else.
- If I get out of bed, I'll have to make it.
- It will save me coming back to bed for a nap later.
- I'll only be back here in 16 hours anyway.
- The more I stay in bed, the less money I spend.
- One less blast of deodorant is good for the planet.
- I've just farted - if I move it will escape.
- I need to rest up for all the things I might do tomorrow.
- If breakfast in bed exists, lunch and dinner in bed can too.

I BOUGHT A LAPTOP FOR A REASON.

I'M GOING FOR THE RECORD FOR 'BED SELFIES'.

I'M PRACTISING HORIZONTAL YOGA.

BELLY LAUGHS

YOU'VE PUT ON A COUPLE OF POUNDS, BUT YOU EAT SALAD EVERY DAY. DEEP-FRIED SALAD?

- There are 365 people in my office so there's birthday cake every day.
- Turns out a 'venti' coffee isn't a small coffee after all.
- I start the day with a bad breakfast and keep on going.
- I can't let food go past the sell-by date.
- I quit smoking, and chips seemed like the ideal substitute.
- I suffered a 'snaccident'.
- I have metal fillings so my fridge magnets keep pulling me back to the kitchen.
- My invisible friend stepped on the scales with me.
- I thought a balanced diet was a pint in each hand.

- I thought vegan was a planet in Star Trek.
- It's an all-you-can-eat buffet - I want my money's worth.

HERBAL REMEDIES

WHEN YOUR HIDDEN STASH IS NO LONGER HIDDEN.

- I'm trying to prevent blindness.
- It's oregano.
- I'm looking after it for your mum.
- I found it in your drawer.
- I'm using it to make ink.
- It was inside the stuffed toy you brought back from Thailand.
- Where's the rest of it?

AT WORK

WHAT DO YOU HATE MOST ABOUT WORK? THE COMMUTE? YOUR BOSS? THE KNOWLEDGE THAT YOU'LL HAVE TO REPEAT THE SAME DAILY GRIND EVERY DAY FOR THE REST OF YOUR LIFE?

You quickly learn how to minimise the amount of work you need to do to survive. By showing up late (if at all), taking a long lunch and going home early, you can easily make a day-long task last for a whole week.

The only problem is your boss. The pesky so-and-so has so many questions about why you're not at your desk, where that report is and why the police are here for you again.

We can't stop you from getting fired, but a few well-chosen excuses might delay the inevitable for just one more day.

BETTER LATE THAN NEVER

THEY SHOULD BE GRATEFUL YOU SHOWED UP AT ALL.

- I saw my ex had broken down and had to drive by them five times before they noticed me laughing.
- I sprayed shaving foam on my armpits instead of deodorant and I had to take another shower.
- So the clocks don't go forward an hour every month?
- I had a game of hide and seek with my nephew and he took hours to find me.
- I got stuck in a Chinese finger trap.
- Someone hacked the traffic lights.
- I was mistaken for Brad Pitt at the train station and spent an hour signing autographs.
- Elvis hid all my shoes.
- My socks were matching so I went home to mix them up because I don't conform to your office stereotype.

- I'm not late. I decided to change my hours to make them more convenient.
- The landlord changed the lock on the garage and I couldn't get to my car.
- A police helicopter hovered over my house blaring 'Stay inside, I repeat, stay inside'.
- I accidentally went to my old job.
- You didn't call to wake me up.

THAT'S ENTERTAINMENT

WHEN IT COMES TO ENTERTAINING YOUR CLIENTS ON EXPENSES, THE CUSTOMER IS ALWAYS RIGHT.

- The client insisted I had a new car.
- The client insisted on three Michelin stars.
- The client insisted on more champagne.
- The client insisted on going to a strip club.
- The client insisted on a weekend in Amsterdam.
- The client insisted on a week in Thailand.

NO JOB, NO PROBLEM

DIDN'T THEY BAN JOB-HUNTING?

- Work does not suit my personality.
- No company can handle this much rock and roll.
- My work/life balance demands 100% life.
- I'm setting up my own business promoting brand 'Me'.
- If I get a job I won't have time for my poetry/band/acting career.
- My skills are so advanced that no one knows how to use them yet.
- It would be selfish of me to get a job when other people need one more than I do.
- I'm waiting for 'King of the World' to become available.
- The right opportunity will find me when it's ready.

DISTRACTION PIECES

GIVE THEM SOMETHING BIGGER TO WORRY ABOUT.

- HR told me you didn't work here any more.
- I think I emailed the figures to our competitor instead.
- You say negligence. I say a breezy outlook on life.
- I didn't have time to work on your project and talk to the Fraud Squad about it.
- I'm sure you asked me to send the payment to a Nigerian prince.
- The safety checks are optional, aren't they?
- The health and safety inspector didn't look happy.
- So what if the stock price has crashed?

NO SHOW

SOME DAYS IT'S NOT WORTH BOTHERING.

- The universe told me to take a day off.
- I set my uniform on fire by putting it in the microwave to dry.
- My 'anal glaucoma' was acting up. I just didn't see my arse getting in today.
- I woke up in a good mood and I didn't want to ruin it.
- All my underwear is in the wash.
- I have to go to the beach – my doctor says it's critical I get more vitamin D.
- I'm handcuffed to the bed and I can't find the key.
- My guinea pig has flu and needs round-the-clock attention.
- I got lucky last night and I'm not sure where I am.
- I left a spoon in my morning coffee and now I'm blind in one eye.
- I worked an extra five minutes every day this month, so I'm due a day off.

YOUR HAIR OFFENDED ME YESTERDAY AND I'M NOT COMING BACK UNTIL YOU CHANGE IT.

MY GLASS EYE FELL OUT AND I CAN'T FIND IT.

MY BODY HASN'T ADJUSTED TO CLIMATE CHANGE.

OFFICE AFFLICTIONS

WHEN A COLD IS NO LONGER ENOUGH.

My doctor says I have a bad case of:

- Screen burn.
- Carpool Tunnel syndrome.
- Netflix and chilblains.
- Acute deadline-itis.
- Attention-to-detail deficit disorder.
- My-cardigan infarction.
- Ingrowing cubicles.
- Tuberculoffice.

TRADESMAN TRICKS

BECAUSE YOUR CUSTOMER IS RARELY RIGHT.

- My van got stolen.
- All it needs is another coat.
- He's new on the team.
- Your planning permission expired.
- Your architect told me to do it like that.
- I thought you wanted it that way.
- The estimate doesn't include that.
- The windows won't show up until next week.
- They don't come in that size.
- We had a pipe burst so we had to go to the other job.

LONG LONG LUNCH

IT'S NOT LIKE YOU DO ANYTHING AT YOUR DESK ANYWAY.

- Someone nicked my parking space.
- I thought it was Saturday lunchtime and forgot to come back to work.
- All my best work is done under the influence of beer.
- I went to pay a cheque into the bank and these men with guns came in and I shouted, 'Not on my lunchbreak' and, well, you'll see the rest on the news later.
- I bumped into Stephen Hawking and couldn't miss the opportunity to find out about absolutely everything.
- There was some white powder on the floor so the canteen went into lockdown for two hours.
- I went to get my hair cut and the hairdresser had sooooo many questions.

CAUGHT RED-HANDED

IF THEY LEAVE THESE THINGS AROUND, WHAT DO THEY EXPECT?

- You said the biscuits were free.
- It's the petty cash tin? I thought it was my tip jar.
- I was using the photocopier to photograph my bottom to show the doctor. Ask *him* why he needs 50 copies.
- I was using Facebook to see what other people thought about the company.
- I took the iPad home to work at the weekend.
- I'm not looking for another job, I was just using my CV to test the printer.

DODGING DEADLINES

THERE ARE MORE IMPORTANT THINGS TO DO THAN WORK.

- They took my favourite meal off the canteen menu. I'm still in mourning.
- There is no excuse for laziness, but if you find one let me know.
- I don't work here, I just like wearing the uniform.
- I know you're a perfectionist and perfection takes time.
- I thought you cancelled that project.
- It sounded dull so I read Bertrand Russell's *In Praise of Idleness* instead.
- I asked Geoff to do it but he refused.
- I couldn't read your handwriting.
- I couldn't work out how to make the numbers uppercase.
- Your email about it went into my spam folder.
- I couldn't decide which font to use.

INSTEAD OF PRINTING THE REPORT, I ACCIDENTALLY PRINTED THE INTERNET INSTEAD.

I DID IT IN MY HEAD AND FORGOT TO WRITE IT DOWN.

I GOT MY TIE CAUGHT IN THE SHREDDER.

iBROKE IT

BECAUSE THERE IS NO APP FOR FIXING A SMASHED PHONE.

- You bought me such a cheap phone, the dog thought it was a chew toy.
- I was holding my phone and a lung for a transplant operation when I tripped. I had to make a choice which hand would break my fall.
- I was so happy when I got a text from you that I dropped it while celebrating.
- I dropped it rescuing a child from a well.
- I used it as a weapon to fend off ninjas.
- No one told me that I couldn't dry it in the microwave.
- My flatmate was drunk, knocked it into the toilet and flushed it.
- I accidentally baked it into a cake I was making for you.
- The spirit level app worked really well. The hammer app less so.
- I lent my phone to you. When can I have it back?

- I had a new phone cover that looked like a fish. It was so convincing, a seagull swooped down and stole it from me.
- Someone changed my ring tone to the sound of a wasp.

BUSINESS TRAVEL BLUES

YOUR BOSS KNOWS YOU ALREADY HAVE ENOUGH TROUBLE FINDING THE OFFICE EVERY DAY.

- I made the flight on time, but it was the wrong one.
- They thought my laptop was a bomb and made me get off the plane.
- Airport security mistook me for a terrorist and detained me.
- I have DDS (Directional Dysfunction Syndrome).
- I didn't choose the Adult Channel - I fell asleep on the remote control.
- It takes me three weeks to get over an hour's jet-lag.

THE BLOKE ON THE STREET CORNER SAID 'TOMORROW IS THE END OF THE WORLD' SO I'M HEADING OFF NOW TO TIDY UP.

WORKING 9 TO 3:30

YOU GOT IN ON TIME. YOU HAD A QUICK LUNCH. SO KNOCK OFF EARLY.

- There's someone coming to read the gas meter.
- It's a full moon. We must gather.
- My daughter is in a school play and if I don't see her, she'll be scarred for life.
- I need to give a blood transfusion to my best friend.
- I'm meeting with my parole officer.
- I'm going home early in solidarity with all the kids working in sweatshops around the world.
- My mother is coming to visit and I need to pick her up at the station.
- My mother is coming to visit and I need to pick up my pills from the chemist.
- My mother is leaving today so I'm heading to the pub.

TECH TRAUMA

NO ONE KNOWS HOW COMPUTERS WORK ANYWAY.

- The internet was down.
- The program crashed.
- I sneezed and gave the computer a virus.
- I spilled couscous on my keyboard.
- The printer was out of ink and I couldn't find the office squid.
- A cat chased away my mouse.
- The temp stole my flash drive.
- Someone smashed my Windows.
- The IT guy refused to turn it off and on again.
- I can't stop my computer auto-correcting everything into French.
- I played Angry Birds too long and sprained my fingers so I couldn't type.

LONG-TERM LARKING

ONE DAY OUT IS EASY. A WHOLE WEEK REQUIRES EFFORT.

- Sorry, I can't tell you due to the injunction.
- Turns out I was on the same programme as Jason Bourne.
- I've been undercover. If I told you anything else, I'd have to kill you.
- I thought I'd won the lottery so I went on holiday by mistake.
- I got snowed in. The snow was out of season and highly localised.
- I've been on jury service - there's a media blackout on the case.
- I've had a tooth out every day for the last week.
- I got stuck in the kettle while I was cleaning it.
- The bus hasn't stopped for me in the last week.
- I won't be in next week because I hate working here.

AT PLAY

HOW MUCH TIME IS LEFT IN THE DAY AFTER YOU HAVE PUT IN THE EFFORT TO COMPLETE (OR SUCCESSFULLY AVOID) ALL OF YOUR DUTIES AT HOME AND AT WORK? NOT ENOUGH. NOT ENOUGH BY FAR.

So those remaining, precious moments should be filled with what you enjoy. But even then you can end up under pressure. You get hassle to look after yourself, be a good friend, behave like a rational human being after ten pints - the list is endless.

You know perfectly well that being a good friend or teammate is hard and it's not always possible to bring your A-game to everything you do socially. Unfortunately, it seems to be the case that your friends and teammates need a gentle reminder sometimes.

CLOSE FRIENDS ONLY

WHEN THEY FIND OUT THEY'VE BEEN UNFRIENDED/UNFOLLOWED/DELETED.

- Sorry, I thought you were dead.
- My phone was running out of space from all your duckface pictures.
- One of my other personalities must have done it.
- You looked so old in your profile photo I thought you were my old geography teacher.
- I need to spend more time talking about you than with you.
- You were confusing 'funny' with 'racist'.
- I'm deleting everyone and creating a new profile – I'll invite you later. Promise.
- I have a colleagues profile and a friends profile. I'm not sure which you are.

GAME OVER

THERE'S ALWAYS TIME FOR ONE MORE GO ON THE X-BOX.

- It's improving my hand–eye co-ordination.
- When the zombie uprising happens, you'll be glad I've been rehearsing.
- It cost so much that if I don't use it, it will be a waste of money. And you hate wasting money.
- This isn't a game, I'm interviewing to be a drone pilot.
- I'm reviewing this for my blog. My followers depend on me.
- Because if I stop now the Kill-troupers will conquer the Realm of Dreamstax and I'll never rescue the Ubermaiden which would cause the collapse of society across the Neo-universe and let the Cho-min from the Parallex dimension cross over and... (until they get bored and go away).

GYM JAMS

GYMS ARE TOO MUCH LIKE HARD WORK, SO DON'T JOIN IN THE FIRST PLACE.

- The world is my gym.
- My physique would intimidate everyone else.
- It would throw off the 'not going to the gym today' streak I've had going my entire life.
- I always have a prior engagement with food.
- Sweat makes my hair frizz up.
- I've already made too many New Year's Resolutions.
- I'm allergic to lycra.
- It's cheaper to have a daily protein shake.

WORKOUT WOES

YOU ACCIDENTALLY JOINED A GYM. NOW YOU REALLY NEED TO STEP IT UP.

- I left my membership card in Stockholm.
- I ate half-fat cheese for lunch, that's enough for one day.
- The clocks went back today so I've already spent an extra hour up and about.
- I visited my friend Jim this morning. That's the same, right?
- I've already showered today. A second shower is a waste of natural resources.
- I'm having a good hair day and I don't want to spoil it.
- Netflix automatically started the next episode of *House of Cards*.
- My sexy workout clothes are in the wash, and what if 'the one' is at the gym today?
- I have a paper cut and if I sweat it might get infected.
- I've forgotten my headphones and the techno they play is not my sound, man.

LOAN ARRANGER

YOUR MATE SHOULDN'T HAVE LENT YOU THE MONEY IN THE FIRST PLACE.

- Here are fifty used scratch cards. Turns out you're quite unlucky.
- I have a new girlfriend and I can't afford anything else.
- I've lost weight recently and I need the money to buy new clothes.
- I used it to buy the last round - you would have done the same.
- I owe Sally £10 as well, and she's bigger than you.
- I bought a load of stamps before the price went up again.
- I paid you back last week - you were drunk at the time.
- I gave it to Pete to give to you.
- I invested it in a 10-year government bond for you. See you in 10 years.

SOCIAL TEDIA

THE LIFE YOU PRETEND TO HAVE ONLINE IS BETTER THAN YOUR REAL ONE.

- I'm tracking the spread of bird flu so we know when to evacuate.
- I'm expecting a new mission from 'Colonel X'.
- I'm setting my homescreen to a picture of you.
- I'm watching a video on how to be a more considerate partner.
- I'm checking the weather to make sure it's ideal for our special day out.
- I'm checking restaurant reviews for a date night treat.
- I'm deleting the rude comments people made about your mother.
- I'm looking through all my pictures of you to remind me how lucky I am.

HOME SWEET HOME

GOING OUT IS NOT ALL IT'S CRACKED UP TO BE.

- My fake tan didn't take.
- My online auction finishes in an hour.
- I'm trying to be less popular.
- Sorry, I think I deleted the email. I must have read 'Birthday Plans' as 'Penis Enlargement'.
- I'm a method actor researching the role of an agoraphobic.
- The world just isn't ready for my dance moves.
- It wouldn't be fair to everyone else who is out on the pull.
- I've already been out once this year.
- I've just put a pie in the oven.
- My windscreen wipers aren't working and it might rain.
- It started to go wrong when I saw a little cake with 'EAT ME' on it...
- I'm observing National 'Don't Go Out At All' Week.

PASSING ON PASSENGERS

TODAY THEY ASK FOR A LIFT. IF YOU SAY YES, TOMORROW THEY ASK YOU TO HELP BURY A BODY.

- My insurance won't cover it.
- The car is due for a service. In exactly five minutes' time.
- My cat died in the front seat and it's now a shrine.
- The tyre pressure is not tuned to accommodate your weight.
- I've just got a job with Uber and this is my day off.
- My sat nav shows a picture of a knife and a gun at your postcode.
- I'm still having the passenger seats dry cleaned after the last time.

A WORD FROM OUR SPONSORS

CHARITY BEGINS IN SOMEONE ELSE'S HOME.

- I gave all my spare cash to the Donkeys with Dandruff Society.
- I bought a lottery ticket instead. I'll give 1% of the winnings to your charity.
- If I pay for your skydive, will you pay for my weekend in Paris?
- My accountant says I gave too much last year.
- I left my wallet in Luxembourg.
- If I give to your charity, it means I'm taking away from all the others. That's your fault.
- I'm sure it's a front for organised crime.

SMOKE SIGNALS

QUITTING IS FOR QUITTERS.

- White teeth are so last year.
- I just bought 100 lighters.
- It would be bad for my exercise regime - I walk to the corner shop every day to buy cigarettes.
- I'm building a new driveway, and I need the tar.
- My dog wouldn't recognise me by smell any more.
- All the posters say it's second-hand smoke that kills you.
- I'm trying to develop a convincing cough so my boss believes me when I call in sick.
- I need something to do while the dog does his business. Otherwise I'm just standing there watching.
- My ashtray collection has sentimental value.
- I know the health implications - I smoke because it's ironic.

ALCO-FROLICS

SERIOUSLY, I'M NOT DRUNK...

- I'm practising a new accent.
- I'm just tired from all the drinking.
- I'm a gravity inspector.
- I'm having a flashback to a rollercoaster ride.
- Aliens kidnapped me and experimented on my body with ethanol.
- There's no law that says you have to walk in a straight line.
- I have a rare condition that makes my legs go weak after being in the presence of alcohol.
- Someone has to check that the cleaner dusted the skirting boards.
- And you can tell your identical twin that too.

THE MORNING AFTER

SERIOUSLY, I'M NOT HUNGOVER...

- I've got a headache from thinking too much.
- It's wine flu.
- I'm still drunk.
- I'm so clever my brain has got too big for my skull.
- I sometimes wear sunglasses indoors to pretend I'm famous.
- Sunlight is never good - I'm half vampire.
- I'm just allergic to Mondays / Tuesdays / Wednesdays / Thursdays / Fridays.
- I've just learnt to hear sunlight.
- It's the Grape Depression.

ABOUT THE NIGHT BEFORE

WHY APOLOGISE WHEN YOU CAN MAKE AN EXCUSE?

- Turns out that 15th beer was off.
- I had temporary amnesia.
- I'm schizophrenic and my other personality is a right sod.
- My evil twin did it.
- I was just following orders.
- I was abducted by aliens.
- I was replaced by a clone.
- The barman wouldn't take no for an answer.

IT'S JUST NOT CRICKET

YOU ARE THE ULTIMATE SPORTSMAN – HOW COULD YOUR POOR PERFORMANCE BE YOUR FAULT?

- I was scared there might be a streaker.
- My teammate put itching powder in my jockstrap.
- The ball was too bouncy.
- That tactic worked much better on the Playstation.
- That net looks higher than last week.
- The grass is the wrong shade of green.
- The referee looked at me in a funny way.
- This looked a lot easier on TV.
- The pitch is on top of an ancient burial ground.
- I had too much sports drink and needed the toilet all the way through the match.
- My new trainers went out of fashion before the game finished.

HOLIDAYS ON HOLD

CANCELLING A HOLIDAY IS LESS EFFORT THAN TAKING IT.

- I didn't book this - my cat did when it walked across my computer.
- I wouldn't have booked a twin room for my children, they aren't twins.
- I've changed my mind - Spain is too Spanish.
- I don't need to go any more - I've found a great fake tan.
- I'm cancelling the honeymoon because we eloped to Vegas last week.
- I hated this hotel when I stayed here in a previous life.
- The hotel name is an anagram of my nemesis.
- I can't decide what to wear.
- Someone that looks like me is on the terrorist watchlist.

- I just watched *Airplane* - I can't risk the same pilot.
- TripAdvisor warned me about drink and drugs - there aren't any.

HAPPY BIRTHDAY TO WHO?

YOU WANTED TO REMEMBER YOUR MATE'S BIRTHDAY - IT'S THE THOUGHT THAT COUNTS.

- I clicked the wrong button and your present was shipped to Bulgaria.
- I thought you were too cool for a bourgeois construct like birthdays?
- Do you really want to be reminded of your age?
- Didn't you have a birthday last year?
- I thought your birthday was the week after your twin sister's?
- I made you a card but it was so good an international art thief stole it.

OFFICIALS

THERE ARE SO MANY RULES AND REGULATIONS IN EVERYDAY LIFE THAT IT'S HARD TO KEEP TRACK OF THEM ALL. AND, FOR SOME REASON, PEOPLE KICK UP A FUSS WHEN YOU DON'T FOLLOW THEM ALL TO THE LETTER.

It was much easier in the old days when there were just ten commandments to follow. Then again, you might be hard pushed to come up with an excuse for why you have coveted your neighbour's ox for the umpteenth time. No matter how brilliant their ox is. (Seriously, it's time for a new ox.)

Even when there's not a hard and fast law involved, there's still a lot expected of you. Appointments to keep, forms to complete, bills to pay - it's a wonder you have time in the day to find enough excuses to fend it all off.

GO FASTER STRIFE

SPEED LIMITS ARE MERELY ADVISORY. AREN'T THEY?

- I was low on petrol – I wanted to make sure I had enough speed to coast home.
- The sign said A85 – I thought that was the speed limit.
- I just had my hair cut, it just makes me look fast.
- I wouldn't have pulled over if I'd known you wanted to criticise me.
- I was trying to get the snow off my windscreen so I could see where I was going.
- I couldn't have been doing 120, my speedometer only goes to 110.
- I had to get home as fast as possible – my insurance runs out at midnight.
- I have a cold and when I sneeze, my foot hits the pedal.
- I need to get to the pub before they stop serving food.

THE JURY'S OUT

VERDICTS ARE DECIDED BY PEOPLE WHO AREN'T SMART ENOUGH TO AVOID JURY SERVICE. JUST SAYING.

- There's a good chance one of my family did it.
- I don't have an outfit that says 'Justice'.
- I've seen every episode of CSI.
- If he's a ginger, he's guilty.
- I've had sex with every judge in this city.
- I've booked a non-refundable holiday in my bedroom.
- I have a tattoo that reads 'Guilty' on my forehead.
- I'm a session bassoon player – I could be required for work at any moment.

GOOD EVENING PINT-STABLE

I'M NOT DRUNK OFFICER. THE EMPTY BOTTLE? OH...

- The whisky must have evaporated.
- Can't you see the genie?
- I'm just taking it to the recycling.
- It's a prop for a play.
- It's a classic design that I'm donating to a museum.
- It was empty when I bought it. I'm taking it back to the shop to complain.
- I used it to top up the radiator.
- Where has the little ship gone?

CREDIT WHERE IT'S DUE

YOU ONLY GROW WHEN YOU PUSH YOUR LIMITS - THAT MUST INCLUDE CREDIT CARD LIMITS.

- I'm colour blind - I can't see red ink.
- I thought the statement was what *you* owed *me*.
- I want to live in a society where money is a thing of the past.
- It's your fault, you sent me the credit card.
- I thought your bill was a scam.
- If you'd asked more politely, I might have sent you the money.
- I chose to give the money to charity rather than an evil corporation like you. When I say charity, I mean scratch cards.
- These are things I bought for my girlfriend. She left me, so let's call it quits.
- I can either pay your bill, the gas bill or the electricity bill. Please get together and let me know which of you deserves it most.

ELECTION REJECTION

DEMOCRACY IS GREAT, BUT VOTING IS JUST A HASSLE.

- It's not my fault the pub is on the way to the polling station.
- I used my vote on *The X-Factor*.
- I like brown. No party has brown as its colour.
- The voting booth sets off my claustrophobia.
- Putting a cross in a box seems very negative.
- There's no free bar.
- I'm waiting to see who's going to win before I decide.
- I've already been told the result by a member of the Illuminati.
- I couldn't vote for myself, so there's really no point.
- I can't vote. I'm the reigning monarch / certified insane / guilty of electoral fraud.
- I'd feel guilty if the person I didn't vote for lost.

LEFTIE DAVE PROMISED NOT TO VOTE AS WELL, SO WE CANCEL EACH OTHER OUT.

I'M NEARLY OUT OF DATA AND THERE'S NO FREE WIFI THERE.

DENTIST DIVERSIONS

WHY BOTHER VISITING THE DENTIST? HE'S OUT PLAYING GOLF ANYWAY.

- All my teeth fell out already.
- I keep having nightmares you'll turn me into the Bond baddie, Jaws.
- I'm in love with you.
- My breath is so bad you might slap me.
- I had an argument with my tooth so I want it to fall out anyway.
- My toothache is so bad I don't want to get out of bed.
- I'm in jail.
- Dentures aren't that expensive.
- I'll chew on the other side.
- Perfect teeth are just a vanity.

DEFERRING THE DOCTOR

THE DOCTOR WON'T SEE YOU NOW.

- These things just go away by themselves.
- I'm sure you have more important patients than me.
- I checked the symptoms on the internet. I'm either fine or I died last week anyway.
- The endoscope is too cold.
- The doctor looks too much like my mother.
- I quite enjoy taking aspirin.
- I vibrate on an astral plane that transcends physical pain.
- Let's just wait until it gets really bad.

I USED THE FORM AS A BOOKMARK AND TOOK THE BOOK BACK TO THE LIBRARY.

GOING POSTAL

THEY'VE HEARD 'IT'S IN THE POST' ALREADY - TIME TO UP YOUR GAME.

- I heard someone set fire to the post box.
- Perhaps you misfiled it?
- I haven't seen it since my trip to Mensa.
- My butler threw it away.
- It was so good that my mum is having it laminated.
- Thinking about it, the post box is next to a large bin.
- You did want me to send it to your Mongolian office?
- Is your postboy a bit light-fingered?
- I'm banned from going within 20 feet of a post box since the mascarpone incident.
- Of course I don't have the original any more. I faxed it to you last week.
- I've already sent it to you six times, please leave me alone!

TERM-TIME TRAVEL

WHAT DOES IT MATTER IF YOUR KIDS MISS LEARNING ABOUT OXBOW LAKES?

- Disneyland is educational, it will allow Mary to research gigantism in mice and ducks.
- We think it's the last time Mary will see Aunt Margaret alive.
- I'll donate the money I save on the hotel to the teachers' benevolent fund.
- It's flu season. We expect Mary to get the flu from the 7th to the 15th.
- We're moving to Thailand. If we don't like it after a week, we'll come back.
- Terrorists will only speak to Mary to discuss the hostage release. Face to face. In Benidorm.

IT PAPER CUTS BOTH WAYS

IF YOU HAVEN'T SEEN THE LETTER/BILL/ FINAL DEMAND, WHAT DO THEY EXPECT?

- It never arrived.
- Next door sometimes get my post.
- The postman hates me.
- I don't have a letterbox.
- The cleaner steals my post.
- The kids keep using the post for their origami models.
- We ran out of toilet paper and...
- I've accidentally had all my post diverted to the bin.
- I've been threatened with a letter bomb so I bury all my post.
- My house doesn't have a name or number for security purposes.

MANY HAPPY RETURNS

SORRY - WE ALREADY KNOW THESE WON'T WORK - THE TAX MAN TAKES NO EXCUSES.

- My sister always completed my returns but we've fallen out.
- My accountant has been ill.
- My dog was ill so I ate my tax return for him.
- I have renounced all worldly goods and so I have nothing to pay tax on.
- After seeing a volcanic eruption on the news, I couldn't concentrate on anything else.
- My flatmate had a nervous breakdown and he used my receipts to make paper dolls.
- I'll be abroad on deadline day with no internet access so I won't be able to file it.
- My niece moved in. She made the house so untidy I couldn't find my log-in details.
- I had an argument with my wife and went to Italy for 5 years.
- I'm from a country where 'Tax Return' means 'men's toilet'.
- Cyborgs!

MY BAD BACK MEANS I CAN'T GO UPSTAIRS. THAT'S WHERE MY TAX RETURN IS.

I'VE BEEN CRUISING ROUND THE WORLD IN MY YACHT, AND ONLY PICKING UP POST WHEN I'M ON DRY LAND.

I'M A DRUID, SO I AM EXEMPT.

I'VE BEEN TOO BUSY SUBMITTING MY CLIENTS' TAX RETURNS.

TRAIN TICKET TRANSGRESSIONS

THINGS SOON GO OFF THE RAILS WHEN YOU DON'T HAVE A TICKET.

- What's a ticket?
- I threw it away because it gave me a papercut. I'm considering legal action.
- Sorry, I'm in a coma.
- I thought tickets were optional.
- My dad is the driver.
- I wasn't sure when I was coming back so I couldn't buy a return.
- I thought the railway was free since 1994.
- I gave it to the other ticket inspector that passed here two minutes ago.
- If the man in the ticket office doesn't see me then I don't need one.
- Can't I ride in the luggage rack for free?
- I jumped the barrier as part of my Olympic training.

GO FASTER STRIFE 2

BECAUSE WE KNOW YOU'LL GET CAUGHT MORE THAN ONCE.

- I've just bought some fancy ice cream and I don't want it to melt before I get it home to my pregnant wife.
- There's a wasp in the car - I thought if I did 100 with the windows open, it would get sucked out.
- I'm auditioning for the next *The Fast and the Furious* film.
- I have 10 minutes to get this sample to the hospital.
- My missus ran away with a police officer the other week and I thought you were bringing her back.
- I was trying to get away from the other policeman.
- It just looked like I was speeding because everyone else was going so slowly.
- I didn't think the speed limit applied after 11pm.

MULTI-PURPOSE

WE'VE DONE OUR BEST TO THINK OF ALL THE KEY MOMENTS WHEN YOU MIGHT NEED AN EXCUSE. BUT YOUR LIFE IS UNIQUE, AND WHILE WE'D LIKE TO TAILOR THE EXCUSES EVEN FURTHER, OUR SPY CAMERAS HAVE BEEN REMOVED FROM YOUR HOUSE BY THE AUTHORITIES. THAT'S OUR EXCUSE, ANYWAY.

So please consider this last chapter a Swiss-army knife. Wherever you are, whatever you're up to, no matter what you're trying to avoid, there is a blade here to help you on your way.

Your instincts will tell you whether it's time for fight or flight. You can pass the buck to someone else or get your sorry self out of there.

Though to be honest, you should have used an excuse not to get into that situation in the first place. Have we taught you nothing?

DAYDREAMING

IF YOU'RE SO BROKE, YOU CAN'T EVEN AFFORD TO PAY ATTENTION TO ANYONE.

- I was trying to guess the wifi password.
- I was thinking about you wrapped in tinfoil with an apple in your mouth.
- I was looking for Jesus in my heart.
- Sorry, I was distracted by that pulsating vein on your forehead.
- I was too busy not paying attention to you.
- I was listening, you just bored one of my ears to death.
- Deciding what to have for lunch was more important.

PASS THE BUCK

TIP: ALWAYS GENERALISE. ALWAYS.

- I blame the economy.
- I blame the government.
- I blame the weather.
- I blame the media.
- I blame my parents.
- I blame the French.
- I blame the 1970s.
- I blame the internet.
- I blame hipsters.

RELATIVELY SPEAKING

SICK RELATIVES ARE THE BEDROCK OF EXCUSES. JUST PICK ONE OF YOUR VASTLY EXTENDED FAMILY TO BE ILL AND NEED HELP AT ANY TIME.

- Mum and dad.
- Stepmum and stepdad.
- Foster mum and dad.
- Brothers and sisters.
- Step brothers and step sisters.
- Grandmothers and grandfathers.
- Great-grandmothers and great-grandfathers.
- Great-great-grandmothers and great-great-grandfathers.
- Uncles and aunts.
- Great-uncles and great-aunts.
- Nieces and nephews.
- Cousins, first cousins, second cousins, third cousins, etc.

- First cousin once removed, first cousin twice removed, etc.
- The lion that raised you in the jungle.

YOU'RE A SAINT

WHEN YOU'RE TOO BUSY HELPING SOMEONE ELSE ALREADY.

- Picking Mum up from the airport.
- Taking Dad to the hospital.
- Looking after the neighbour's dog.
- Picking your nephew up from school.
- Helping Gran move.
- Serving at the soup kitchen.
- Teaching blind children braille.
- Rescuing endangered fluffy kittens.
- Advising the Prime Minister on community issues.
- Finding a path to world peace.

SLEEPING BEAUTY

WHY SHOULD THE WORD 'OVERSLEEP' SOUND NEGATIVE?

- I forgot to buy an alarm clock.
- I forgot to set my alarm clock.
- My alarm clock was not plugged in.
- My radio alarm was set to the Chillout channel.
- My alarm clock was recalled.
- The relaxation tape I used to go to sleep works too well.
- Someone sewed velcro on to my duvet.
- I don't want to risk sleep deprivation.
- You don't want me to risk falling asleep at the wheel do you?

HEALTH STEALTH

WANT A QUICK WAY OUT WITH NO MORE QUESTIONS? ONLY YOUR DOCTOR KNOWS THE TRUTH.

- Out of my way – diarrhoea!
- My sister is going into labour.
- I have to see the doctor about my blood test irregularity.
- I need to take a salt bath to ease my haemorrhoids.
- Is it normal for your tongue to go black?
- I've injured myself during sex.
- I would show you the rash but it's against the law for you to demand to see it.
- I have to get my mother out of rehab.
- I'll show up if you insist, but you'll be liable for the fumigation costs afterwards.
- Constipation has made me a walking time bomb.

PUNCTUAL PROBLEMS

BECAUSE TIME IS RELATIVE NO MATTER WHAT YOU ARE LATE FOR.

- I thought I saw Amy Winehouse in Costa's.
- I was teaching my dog German.
- I let in some Jehovah's Witnesses and they wouldn't leave.
- I super-glued my eye thinking it was contact lens solution.
- I was taking an online survey and I lost track of the time.
- My trousers split on the way here.
- My left indicator was broken so I had to make right turns all the way here.
- I fell asleep in the shower.
- There was a wasp in my bedroom so I hid under my bed for three hours until it went away.
- The trouble with being punctual is that nobody's there to appreciate it.

- I feel like I'm in everyone's way if I show up on time.
- I dropped my glass eye down the drain and I have to wait for someone else to retrieve it for me.
- I was waiting for my deodorant to dry.
- While rowing across the river to get here, I got lost in the fog.
- I was dreaming about football and it went into overtime.
- Someone was following me, and I drove all around town trying to lose them.
- My watch was set to Tokyo time.
- I was trying to get my gun back from the police.
- We had our driveway re-tarred so I couldn't get my car out until it dried.
- I saw a fire engine on the way here and went home to make sure my house wasn't on fire.
- I was losing my mind this morning. It took me half an hour to find it.
- I just found out that I was switched at birth.
- I'm too upset because someone unfriended me on Facebook.

EXCUSES, EXCUSES

A FINAL SET OF ALL-PURPOSE ONE-LINERS TO HELP YOU BE SOMEWHERE ELSE.

- I was up all night arguing with God.
- I saw a particularly ugly baby and had to sit down.
- I was sitting on the loo and my legs fell asleep.
- I got stuck in the blood pressure machine at the chemist and couldn't get out.
- It's more complicated than Facebook privacy settings.
- I got arrested. Not to worry, just not allowed within 150 metres of a supermaket anymore.
- I can't get a babysitter for my pet crickets.
- I have eye problems – I just can't see myself going.
- My flatmate dried his socks in the toaster and started a fire.
- I thought your invitation was sarcastic.
- I was swimming too fast and bumped my head on the poolside.

- My handbrake broke and the car rolled down the hill into an elephant.
- I put some Miracle Grow on houseplants and, well, you know *The Day of the Triffids*?
- My car ran out of petrol and I got a hernia from pushing it.
- My cat looked at me funny.
- The radio's broken in my car and I can't drive without my beats.
- Chapstick and glue look very similar, don't they?
- We're trying for a baby and the doctor says tonight is our best chance.
- I don't have money for petrol because Cash Convertors is closed.
- My girlfriend's husband is dying and I have to be there to console her.
- I'm sorry, Gotham needs me.
- I thought it was the weekend.
- I'll be celebrating Ugandan Independence Day.
- I just got a new leather couch and I was afraid my cat might scratch it.